Do You KNOW?™

THE MICHIGAN WOLVERINES

S0-BCK-606

A hard-hitting quiz for tailgaters, referee-haters, armchair quarterbacks, and anyone who'd kill for their team

Guy Robinson

SOURCEBOOKS, INC.®
NAPERVILLE, ILLINOIS

Published by Sourcebooks, Inc.
P.O. Box 4410, Naperville, Illinois 60567-4410
(630) 961-3900
Fax: (630) 961-2168
www.sourcebooks.com

Printed and bound in the United States of America
SP 10 9 8 7 6 5 4 3 2 1

This is the kind of quiz that will make you dig deep into the football compartment of your brain. If you *really* know the Wolverines and their history, you'll be able to answer questions about classic games you were lucky enough to see while they happened, historic series you've watched on DVD, and unbelievable plays you've heard about so often you've come to think you were on the field yourself. You'll know about winning coaches and losing coaches, celebrated passers and legendary runners, thrilling bowl games and enduring records, special rivalries and favorite traditions—the stuff of countless game days and time afterward sitting around arguing about whether he ever should've gone for the Hail Mary and whose defense was *really* impenetrable.

You should find that some of the answers pop readily to mind. Others will be a true challenge. And however good you think you are, you can expect to face a few that will stop you cold. That's part of the fun.

So here are 100 questions. Count ten points for each correct answer. Where a question has more than one part, you'll be told how to divide the credit. Here and there you'll find a chance to earn five or ten bonus points, so it's theoretically possible to score more than 1,000. (But you won't!)

Figure your performance this way:

Above 900:	**Spectacular!**
700–899:	A very solid showing.
500–699:	Nothing to be ashamed of.
Below 500:	Told you it was tough.

1. As the Wolverines take the field at the start of each game in Michigan Stadium, they jump and touch a banner. What does the banner say? Ten points for the main message, ten bonus points for the line printed underneath.

   " _____ "

2. What's Tim Biakabutuka's full first name?

   a. Timothy
   b. Timora

   c. Tshimanga
   d. Tiakabutuka

3. The surface of the Big House is:

   a. Grass
   b. FieldTurf

   c. AstroTurf
   d. Tartan Turf

4. On November 18, 2006, just before kickoff at the Michigan-Ohio State game, a video memorial tribute to an OSU alumnus was shown at the Horseshoe in Columbus. What alum—it was a master's degree—would that be? (Hint: Some folks were surprised that Ohio authorities would honor him and that Ohio fans would applaud when it was done.)

   _____

5. I was a triple-threat for the Wolverines from 1938 to 1940. I won all sorts of honors wearing my Michigan No. 98, and then had a brief NFL career and a longer life as a sportscaster. One of my sons was a UCLA quarterback but became better known as an actor. In fact, you probably know several of my kids and grandkids by their show biz activities. Who am I?

   _____

6. For years, he honked it three times for a TD, twice for a safety, and once for an extra point. Who was he and what did he honk?

_____

_____

7. Lloyd Carr's first game as interim head coach, in 1995, pitted the Wolverines against the Cavaliers of Virginia. As time remaining on the clock passed the 12-minute mark, Michigan was down 17–0. Then what happened? (For five bonus points, name the quarterback playing in his first game as a Wolverine that day.)

_____

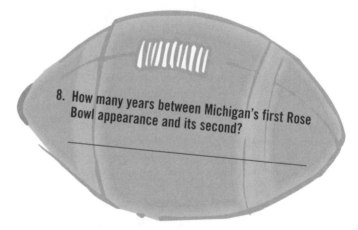

8. How many years between Michigan's first Rose Bowl appearance and its second?

_____

9. As every Wolverine watcher should know, both of those early Rose Bowl games—the first against Stanford, the second against USC—ended with Michigan in the Win column. For five points each, what were the scores of those games?

Michigan v. Stanford: _____

Michigan v. USC: _____

10. The 1992 team compiled a 9–0–3 record. Which three of these opponents fought the Wolverines to a tie? Ten points for all three, five points for two, nothing if you can name only one.

    a. Notre Dame
    b. Alabama
    c. Ohio State
    d. South Carolina
    e. Illinois

11. In one notable contest in 1950, the Wolverines made just nine pass attempts—and failed at all nine. They punted 24 times and didn't gain even one first down. And the other guys—Ohio State—had an even harder time! The score at the half was the final score: 9–3 Michigan. If you know what the game came to be called, that'll explain all.

    _____

12. For five points each, who carried these nicknames?

    a. "Hurry Up": _____
    b. "A-Train": _____

13. What's Jumbo Elliott's given name? _____

14. Which coach won more national titles—Bump Elliott, Bo Schembechler, or Gary Moeller?

    _____

15. The last Michigan football coach to have more than one undefeated season was Harry Kipke, who could boast *three*: 1930, 1931, and 1932. All but one of the six head coaches who followed him had one season without a loss. Which coach was that?

    a. Fritz Crisler
    b. Bennie Oosterbaan
    c. Bump Elliott
    d. Bo Schembechler
    e. Gary Moeller
    f. Lloyd Carr

16. Complete this series of quarterly scores from a certain game held on September 1, 2007. (Hint: A lot of folks back in North Carolina had a pretty happy September.)

    14–7, 17–28, 26–31… _____

17. Name the Wolverine standouts who were All-America choices three years in a row.

    a. 1925, 1926, 1927: _____
    b. 1980, 1981, 1982: _____

18. I was born while my father, an ex-Wolverine, was playing for the Houston Oilers. I too played for Michigan—I set records for receptions, yards, and touchdowns, and made three TD catches against Texas in the 2005 Rose Bowl. (It wasn't enough.) Who am I?

    _____

19. Another Wolverine father-son combination. The father was a fullback at the start of Bennie Oosterbaan's reign; he scored the two comeback TDs that beat California in the 1951 Rose Bowl. The son—same name, but with a "Jr."—was team captain and an All-American in the mid-'70s, and went on to play for the Seattle Seahawks. If you know that their first name was Don, can you give their last?

   _____

20. Michigan used to bring an actual wolverine to football games so fans could have a real mascot, like other teams. True or false?

   _____

21. Probably Michigan's most statistically impressive teams were those of 1901–05, which were dubbed the "Point a Minute" teams. The combined record of those five years was 55–1–1. By how much did they outscore their opponents?

   a. 1,704–236
   b. 2,414–199
   c. 2,821–42
   d. 2,888–376

22. Why was Gary Moeller asked to resign before the start of what would have been his sixth season as head coach?

   _____

   _____

23. **Which coach takes credit for the Wolverines' wings-'n'-stripes design of their helmets? (Ten bonus points for naming the Ivy League school the coach had come from, where he had introduced an earlier version of the new look.)**

    a. Bump Elliott
    b. Fritz Crisler
    c. Harry Kripke
    d. Elton Wieman

24. **It wasn't all about style. Why did he say the design would help his players?**

    _____

25. **Ron Kramer, the Michigan basketball team's starting center, was also a Wolverine two-time All-American end; after his final season he was picked in the first round of the NFL draft by:**

    a. The Detroit Lions
    b. The Green Bay Packers
    c. The Chicago Bears
    d. The New York Giants

26. **Within two, what year did Michigan first play Ohio State? A correct call will get you five points. Want the other five? Get the score. Precisely.**

    The year: _____
    The score: _____

27. In 1973, Michigan and Ohio State, both undefeated, met on a rainy November day in Ann Arbor and stalemated at 10–10. Big Ten directors of athletics voted on which team would represent the conference at the Rose Bowl. How'd the vote turn out? (Five bonus points: Who won the bowl game?)

_____

28. In the fourth quarter of that 10–10 match, a key Wolverine player was injured. Who?

D_____ F_____

29. Here are the scores of five games in the longstanding Michigan-Ohio State rivalry—each a shutout. For two points each, match the scores to the years.

    a. Ohio State 7, Michigan 0   f. 1976
    b. Michigan 10, Ohio State 0   g. 1960
    c. Michigan 22, Ohio State 0   h. 1993
    d. Ohio State 28, Michigan 0   i. 1962
    e. Michigan 28, Ohio State 0   j. 1964

30. Who was the blocking back for Tom Harmon who later coached the Iowa Hawkeyes in the '50s?

_____

31. What happened at the end of the 1998 Rose Bowl to the delight of Michigan and the consternation of the Washington State Cougars and their supporters? (Ten bonus points for the score.)

_____

_____

32. During the recap of the 1968 Ohio State game, Woody Hayes was asked why, after the day's final touchdown brought them to a 50–14 lead, he had ordered his men to go for two. And Hayes, according to tradition, replied:

"_____"

33. The new coach's first year was a doozy: a perfect 9–0 record and a national title. Which coach?

_____

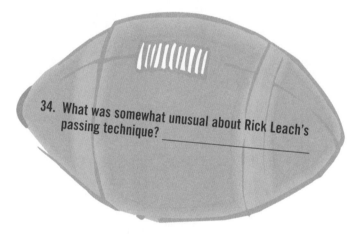

34. What was somewhat unusual about Rick Leach's passing technique? _____

35. In the Orange Bowl that followed the 1999 season, in which Michigan beat Alabama 35–34 in overtime, Tom Brady threw for:

   a. five touchdowns
   b. four touchdowns
   c. two touchdowns
   d. zero touchdowns

36. In the 1979 Michigan-Notre Dame game, how did a Golden Domer defend against what might have been a game-winning 42-yard field goal? (Ten bonus points if you know his name.)

_____

_____

37. Anthony Carter left school with a slew of career records. In which of these categories did he top Michigan's lists? (More than one.)

   a. Receptions
   b. Receiving yards
   c. Touchdowns
   d. Punt returns
   e. Kickoff returns

38. Which line *isn't* in the lyrics to "The Victors," Michigan's fight song?

   a. *Hail! to the victors Valiant!*
   b. *Hail! to the conqu'ring heroes!*
   c. *Here they come, hurrah!*
   d. *The leaders and best!*

39. Who *wasn't* a quarterback?

   a. Bob Timberlake
   b. Jim Harbaugh
   c. John Navarre
   d. Harry Kipke

40. At one time or another, in addition to serving as head football coach at Michigan, Bennie Oosterbaan held each of these positions save one. Which job *didn't* he hold?

   a. Head basketball coach
   b. Freshman baseball coach
   c. Director of athletic alumni relations
   d. Director of athletics

41. Why did Bob Ufer pronounce it "MEE-chigan"?

_____

42. One of the iconic Ufer's best remembered radio calls is of a play
    well recalled by anyone who was there—and, after years of telling
    and retelling, by some who *weren't*: the pass-and-run in a game's
    final six seconds to break a 21–21 tie at the homecoming game of
    1979. For five points each, what freshman made the run and what
    team was the victim? (Ten extra points if you can name the
    quarterback who made the accurate pass.)

_____
_____

43. Five points for naming Michigan's first two Heisman Trophy
    winners, and five more for saying, within two, how many years
    between their two awards. (Five bonus points for telling how many
    years between Heisman No. 2 and Heisman No. 3.)

_____
_____

44. Can you give the first names of the three Wistert brothers, who
    were all superstar tackles for the Wolverines in the '30s and '40s?
    Take ten points for getting all three, five points for two, and
    nothing for just one.

_____
_____
_____

45. The three Wisterts each wore number:

    a. 11   c. 22
    b. 13   d. 24

46. Who grabbed his *third* touchdown pass in triple overtime to clinch a win for Michigan over Michigan State in 2004?

_____

47. What was Bo Schembechler's actual first name?

_____

48. How about Fritz Crisler? What was *his* given name?

_____

49. Desmond Howard famously struck a "Heisman pose" in the end zone after returning a 41-yard punt for a TD against what opponent?

_____

50. Who was Tom Brady's backup at quarterback in 1998 and 1999? (Five bonus points if you know what the backup did for a living for a couple of years before he joined the Dallas Cowboys.)

    D_____ H_____

51. What Wolverine quarterback had to deal with a rowdy fan who ran out of the California stands and tried to tackle him in the middle of an 86-yard touchdown run as Michigan beat the California Bears?

_____

52. Michigan against Stanford at the Rose Bowl, 1902. With eight minutes to play, the score is Michigan 49, Stanford zip. The Cardinal captain approaches his Michigan counterpart and says:

    a. "Please, take it easy out there, will you?"
    b. "We'll get you next time, you can count on it."
    c. "Can you tell me the score?"
    d. "If you are willing, sir, we'll call it a day."

53. Who's Jeff Smoker, and what did he do to the Wolverines in 2001? (Five extra points if you can remember his partner.)

_____

_____

54. What Big Ten Conference rule change resulted from that event?

_____

_____

55. Can you name the Colorado Buffaloes QB whose game-winning Hail Mary pass in the Big House in 1994, with six seconds on the clock, came to be called "The Miracle at Michigan"?

_____

56. Many followers of Michigan football date the Wolverines' comeback after a less than stellar period in the '60s to the defeat of the heavily favored Ohio State in 1969, Bo Schembechler's first year. Score, please?

_____

57. When did Michigan play its first football game?

    a. 1869
    b. 1879
    c. 1889
    d. 1898

58. On the last play of the Michigan-Ohio State game of 1958, a fullback took a hit and dropped what was nearly a game-winning touchdown ball, letting the opponents convert a lead to a win. Who won? (Take 20 bonus points if you can come up with the name of the fullback who fumbled.)

_____

59. What name was given to the undefeated 1947 Wolverines (10–0, plus a Rose Bowl win)?

    a. "The Super-Stalwarts"
    b. "Michigan's Finest"
    c. "The Mad Magicians"
    d. "Crisler's Creatures"

60. How about the 1942 Wolverine line?

    a. "The Seven Oak Posts"
    b. "The Michigan Maulers"
    c. "Sons of Samson"
    d. "Crisler's Crunchers"

61. Which statement about Charles Woodson _isn't_ true?

    a. He didn't play football in high school.
    b. He started for Michigan early in his freshman year.
    c. He was chosen "Big Ten Freshman of the Year."
    d. He won the Heisman Trophy as a junior.

62. At midfield at the Big House is printed a large maize "M." At one end of the field: "MICHIGAN." What's at the other end?

    a. "WOLVERINES"
    b. "MICHIGAN"
    c. "FOOTBALL"
    d. Nothing

63. In the 1991 win over Notre Dame, off a fourth and inches, Desmond Howard made a diving catch into the end zone to secure a 24–14 victory. Who tossed to him?

    _____

64. Ron Johnson did it in 1968. Tim Biakabutuka did it on a Saturday in 1995. Did what?

    _____

65. Fill in the blanks for two points apiece:

    a. _____ described the Big House as "the hole that b. _____ dug, c. _____ paid for, d. _____ carpeted, and e. _____ fills up every Saturday."

66. How tall is Desmond Howard?

    a. 5' 9"
    b. 5' 11"
    c. 6' 2"
    d. 6' 5"

67. What Wolverine superstar was a pilot in the Pacific during World War II and was shot down and listed as missing twice?

_____

68. After his Michigan days, which pro team *didn't* quarterback Jim Harbaugh play with?

   a. Baltimore Ravens
   b. Carolina Panthers
   c. Chicago Bears
   d. Indianapolis Colts
   e. New York Giants
   f. San Diego Chargers

69. The first televised Michigan football game was a 55–0 thrashing of Michigan State. In what year? _____

70. I started my college career at Wisconsin, but it was wartime and eventually, thanks to the Navy V-12 program, I ended up at Michigan. I played two seasons with the Wolverines, eventually making it to the College Football Hall of Fame, while also playing basketball, competing in the broad jump, and pitching for the baseball varsity. I went on to the pros and spent a dozen years as a record-setting running back, again reaching Hall of Fame status. Thanks to a load of publicity, a movie about my life (in which I played myself), and a great nickname, I became better known than most football stars. Who was I?

_____

71. I also got to Michigan through the V-12 program. There, I played football with my brother, Pete. He was a quarterback, I was at right halfback. Both of us later coached major college football teams. Who am I?

_____

72. One more from the World War II era: He started at Michigan in 1944, broke for military service, and returned in 1946 to share left halfback chores with Bob Chappuis. Eventually he shifted to being a return specialist. Who was he?

G_____ D_____

73. Why does Michigan Stadium's official seating capacity always end in 1?

_____

74. In a span of nearly seven decades, from 1910 through 1978, Michigan and Notre Dame met on the gridiron just twice—during a brief thaw in 1942 and 1943. What is generally considered the spark that set off the long blank in the rivalry record?

_____

75. For five points each, who won the games in '42 and '43?

'42: _____
'43: _____

76. Name the center and MVP of the 1934 Wolverines, who gained greater fame in the world of politics.

_____

77. Part of the Michigan pre-game ritual calls for the band's drum major to run to the north end zone, toss his baton over the goalpost, and catch it. According to the long-standing superstition, what's supposed to happen if he misses the catch?

_____

78. "Benny to Bennie" was the combination of what All-American passer and his favorite receiver, future coach Bennie Oosterbaan?

_____

79. Dan Dierdorf, an offensive lineman, was a consensus All-American choice in 1970 and a member of the College Football Hall of Fame. He was picked in the second round of the NFL draft by the team he'd serve for 13 seasons before moving on to a broadcast career. What team?

_____

80. "Football games aren't won—they're lost." Who said it?

    a. "Crazy Legs" Hirsch   c. Tim Tebow
    b. Lloyd Carr   d. Fielding Yost

81. What did Woody Hayes call the University of Michigan?

"_____"

82. In the "Ten-Year War" between Woody and Bo, who won, and by how many games?

_____

83. What trophy is awarded to the winner of the Michigan-Minnesota game?

_____

84. How about the prize traded back and forth in the series between Michigan and Michigan State?

_____

85. Where was Bo during his team's first Rose Bowl appearance, January 1, 1970? (For five bonus points, who'd they face and how'd they do?)

_____

86. How far behind was Michigan at the start of the fourth quarter in the 2003 Little Brown Jug contest, before the astounding rally that resulted in a 38–35 win?

_____

87. In that game, who kicked the 33-yard winning field goal to win?

_____

88. What two Wolverines made the cover of *Time* magazine, eight years apart?

_____

_____

89. By tradition, during key plays at the Big House thousands of fans in the Michigan stands:
    a. Hold their breath
    b. Get up on their seats
    c. Jingle their keys
    d. Do the Wave

90. It happened to Mark Messner four times. It happened to Steve Hutchinson four times, too. What?

_____

91. Coach Harry Kipke did it when he was a Wolverine halfback in the '20s. Anthony Carter did it. So did Derrick Alexander and David Terrell. Braylon Edwards, too. Did what?

_____

92. A 1941 movie tells the story of a legendary Wolverine (who plays himself). For five points, fill in the blank to name the movie, and for five more, what teammate of the star also plays himself?

   a. _____ *of Michigan*
   b. F_____ E_____

93. How did Bo Schembechler do against Notre Dame under Ara Parseghian, his old college teammate from Miami University and former boss at Northwestern?

_____

94. Michigan Stadium is a slightly altered model of what Eastern football facility?

_____

95. Which of these Wolverine stars of the past *wasn't* elected to *both* the College and Pro Football Hall of Fame?

   a. Dan Dierdorf   c. Elroy Hirsch
   b. Benny Friedman   d. Ron Kramer

96. In his seven years coaching West Virginia, before coming to Michigan, how many winning seasons did Rich Rodriguez have?

   a. none   c. 5
   b. 2   d. 6

97. After the 1947 season, the AP writers poll named Notre Dame No. 1 in the country. Shortly after that, the AP ran a second poll; this time Michigan won. Why?

_____

98. Tim Biakabutuka was drafted in the first round by the:

_____

99. Who sniped at a former Michigan Wolverine star by saying, "The trouble with him is he played too many years without a helmet"? Five points for the speaker, five for the object of his derision.

_____
_____

100. How do the musicians in the Michigan Marching Band change their appearance after a Wolverine victory?

   a. They loosen their neckties.
   b. They put "Wolverines Rule" stickers on their foreheads.
   c. They turn their hats around.
   d. They take off their shoes.

ANSWERS

1. GO BLUE
   M CLUB SUPPORTS YOU

2. c.

3. b. (since 2003)

4. Bo Schembechler, who had died the day before

5. Tom Harmon

6. Bob Ufer, the longtime play-by-play man for the Michigan Football Network, let forth blasts on what he described as a horn that came from General George S. Patton's combat jeep

7. What happened is that Michigan scored three times, the final touchdown coming in the last seconds of the game, for a stunning 18–17 comeback win (bonus: the quarterback behind all three scoring drives, including the final 15-yarder to Mercury Hayes, was freshman Scott Dreisbach)

8. From 1902 to 1947 is 45 years

9. The score of both games was 49–0

10. a., c., and e.

11. "The Snow Bowl" (played in Columbus in the wake of a two-day snowstorm that left the field a tough place to hold a football game)

12. a. early-20th-century coach Fielding Yost, b. late-20th-century running back Anthony Thomas

13. John

14. None of them won a national title

15. c. (his closest was 1964, when the team finished 9–1–0)

16. ... 32–34 (the last being the final score of the David-and-Goliath-style shock perpetrated on Michigan by the I-AA team from Appalachian State)

17. a. Bennie Oosterbaan, b. Anthony Carter

18. Braylon Edwards (son of Stan Edwards, who played during the mid-Bo era)

19. Dufek

20. True—both live and stuffed, but not for many decades (guys dressed in wolverine suits don't count)

21. c.

22. He was arrested after a dustup at a restaurant in which he was accused of a drunken assault on a police officer

23. b. (bonus: Princeton)

24. He argued that the new look—replacing the plain black helmets of yore—would help Michigan quarterbacks find their receivers in the downfield crowd

25. b.

26. 1897; Michigan won 34–0

27. Ohio State (bonus: the Buckeyes beat USC 42–21)

28. Quarterback Dennis Franklin

29. a.-g., b.-j., c.-f., d.-i., e.-h.

30. Forest "Evy" Evashevski

31. Out of timeouts and hoping to get off one more play before the clock zeroed his team out of the game, the Cougar quarterback spiked the ball—but not in time, officials ruled (bonus: 21–16)

32. "'Cause I couldn't go for three."

33. That would be Bennie Oosterbaan

34. He threw left-handed

35. b.

36. By climbing onto a mass of men and blocking the ball from the top of the pile (bonus: Bob Crable)

37. All of them

38. c.

39. d. (Kipke was a halfback and punter)

40. d.

41. He was copying the way the word was said by Fielding Yost

42. Anthony Carter, hit on the 20, squirmed past three defenders to beat Indiana (bonus: John Wangler)

43. Tom Harmon in 1940, Desmond Howard in 1991; you do the math (bonus: Charles Woodson in 1997—math again)

44. "Whitey" (Francis), "Moose" (Alvin), and "Ox" (Albert)

45. a.

46. Braylon Edwards

47. Glenn

48. Herbert

49. Ohio State (1991)

50. Drew Henson (bonus: he played professional baseball)

51. Tom Harmon, in a 1940 game; the fan missed the takedown

52. d.

53. In the last seconds of the Michigan State game, he spiked the ball to stop the clock, and then, with the clock reading one second remaining, tossed a short pass to give the Spartans the win (extra points: running back T. J. Duckett, who caught Smoker's pass)

54. After Michigan argued that the timekeeper, a Michigan State employee, managed the clock to give his team the edge, the Conference—although conceding no wrong in this case—changed the rules to require a neutral timekeeper on the field

55. Kordell Stewart

56. 24–12

57. b.

58. Ohio State (bonus: Gene Sisinyak of Michigan)

59. c.

60. a.

61. a.

62. b.

63. Elvis Grbac

64. Rushed for more than 300 yards in a game (Johnson had 347 against Wisconsin, Tim 313 against Ohio State)

65. a. (Radio broadcaster Bob) Ufer, b. (coach Fielding) Yost, c. (coach Fritz) Crisler, d. (athletics director Don) Canham, e. (coach Bo) Schembechler

66. a.

67. Tom Harmon

68. e.

69. 1947

70. Elroy "Crazy Legs" Hirsch

71. Bump Elliott

72. Gene Derricotte

73. The "extra" is Fritz's seat—a mystery place traditionally counted in the stadium tally in honor of Fritz Crisler, former coach and director of athletics

74. A far-reaching coaches' feud between Fielding Yost and Knute Rockne

75. '42: Michigan (32–20), '43: Notre Dame (35–12)

76. Gerald R. Ford

77. The Wolverines will lose the game

78. Benny Friedman

79. The St. Louis Cardinals

80. d.

81. "That school up north"

82. It was 5 for Bo, 4 for Woody, and 1 tie

83. The Little Brown Jug

84. The Paul Bunyan Trophy

85. In the hospital, having suffered a heart attack (bonus: with defensive coordinator Jim Young subbing for him, the team lost to USC, 10–3)

86. Minnesota led by 28–7

87. Garrett Rivas

88. Tom Harmon (1939) and Bob Chappuis (1947)

89. c.

90. Both received All–Big Ten honors four years in a row, Messner 1985–1988 and Hutchinson 1997–2000

91. Wore Jersey No. 1

92. *Harmon of Michigan*, Forest Evashevski

93. Parseghian had left Notre Dame by the time the Irish and the Wolverines picked up their old rivalry, so the two coaches never faced each other

94. Yale Bowl

95. d.

96. d.

97. Between the two votes, Michigan had soundly beaten USC in the Rose Bowl

98. Carolina Panthers

99. Lyndon Johnson said it about Gerald Ford

100. c.